THE U.S. GOVERNMENT
HOW IT WORKS

THE
SENATE

THE U.S. GOVERNMENT
HOW IT WORKS

★ ★ ★

THE CENTRAL INTELLIGENCE AGENCY
THE DEPARTMENT OF HOMELAND SECURITY
THE FEDERAL BUREAU OF INVESTIGATION
THE HOUSE OF REPRESENTATIVES
THE PRESIDENCY
THE SENATE
THE SUPREME COURT

THE U.S. GOVERNMENT
HOW IT WORKS

THE
SENATE

JANET ANDERSON

An imprint of Infobase Publishing

The Senate

Chelsea House
An imprint of Infobase Publishing
132 West 31st Street
New York, NY 10001

ISBN-10: 0-7910-9291-7
ISBN-13: 978-0-7910-9291-0

Library of Congress Cataloging-in-Publication Data
Anderson, Janet, 1952–
  The Senate / Janet Anderson.
      p. cm.—(The U.S. government: how it works)
  Includes bibliographical references and index.
  ISBN 0-7910-9291-7 (hardcover)
 1. United States. Congress. Senate—Juvenile literature. I. Title. II. Series.

 JK1276.A25 2007
 328.73'071—dc22

                                                            2006028585

Chelsea House books are available at special discounts when purchased in bulk quantities for businesses, associations, institutions, or sales promotions. Please call our Special Sales Department in New York at (212) 967–8800 or (800) 322–8755.

You can find Chelsea House on the World Wide Web at http://www.chelseahouse.com

Series design by James Scotto-Lavino
Cover design by Ben Peterson

Printed in the United States of America

BANG NMSG 10 9 8 7 6 5 4 3 2 1

This book is printed on acid-free paper.

All links and Web addresses were checked and verified to be correct at the time of publication. Because of the dynamic nature of the Web, some addresses and links may have changed since publication and may no longer be valid.

CONTENTS

1

A New Nation and a New Government

On March 4, 1789, church bells and cannons rang out in New York City, the first capital of the newly constituted United States. The entire city was celebrating. A new federal government was about to be set in motion, a government of the people, for the people, and by the people.

The Senate and the House of Representatives, the two legislative bodies of the new bicameral (two-house) legislature, were preparing to conduct their first order of business—certifying the election of George Washington as president. Then, the historic first presidential

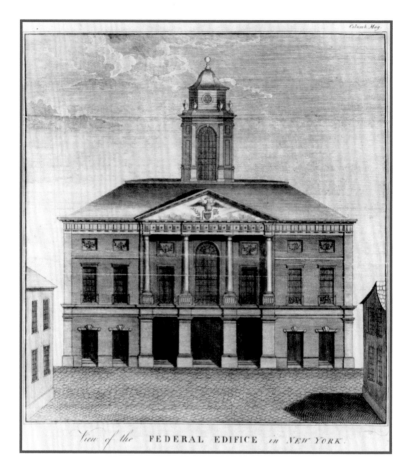

The United States Senate first met in 1789 in the new Federal Hall in New York City. The first meeting of the Senate was to be on March 4, but poor weather kept many senators away. The Senate did not achieve a quorum until April 6.

inauguration would be able to take place. The ceremony would be held in the Senate chamber, the so-called Upper House, but it would include the full House of Representatives as well.

Unfortunately, not enough senators or representatives were present to certify the election. With two senators representing each of the 11 states that had ratified the new Constitution, the first Senate had 22 senators. (Neither Rhode Island nor North Carolina had ratified the Constitution yet.) In order to do business, the Senate needed only a quorum (one-half of its membership, plus one) present, but it did not have the required number of senators in New York City.

It was early spring, and the weather remained troublesome. New England still had snow, and heavy rains had fallen elsewhere. Roads were muddy and treacherous, so travel by horse or coach was slow. Traveling by water was the fastest method of transportation, but it too was subject to problems with the weather as well as mechanical delays.

ELECTORAL VOTES CONFIRMED

It was not until April 6, 1789, that the necessary 12 members were assembled in New York. On that date in an upper chamber of New York's splendid new Federal Hall, the United States Senate was convened for the first time under Vice President John Adams. (Under the Constitution, the vice president serves as president of the Senate.) Its first official task was to count the presidential electoral votes from each state and to certify the election.

The electoral votes were duly counted, and the Senate officially confirmed George Washington's election as president of the United States, a fact already well known

in the new nation. Washington had lingered at his planta-
tion home of Mount Vernon. A congressional delegation
was dispatched to Virginia to ensure that the new president knew his election was official and to encourage his
prompt arrival so that the new government could begin
to operate.

Washington, however, who was also a farmer, found
the pleasures of his Virginia estate and his family hard to
leave behind. After all, he had represented Virginia at the
First and Second Continental Congresses, during which
the 13 colonies struggled to construct a system to unify
their efforts to separate from Great Britain. He led the
Continental Army from 1775 to 1783 and won the victory
at Yorktown, which ended the fighting in the Revolutionary War.

The Articles of Confederation had been approved a year
after the Continental Congress adopted the Declaration of
Independence in 1776; the Articles of Confederation were
intended to provide the legal framework for the 13 colonies embarked on revolution. When the Articles proved
to be an inadequate governing tool after independence,
Washington held a conference in 1785 at Mount Vernon
to consider alternatives. After that gathering proved inef-
fective, he attended another meeting the following year in
Annapolis, Maryland.

It took the persuading of his many friends to get
Washington to Philadelphia the next year for the Constitutional Convention. Reluctantly, he agreed to preside
over the Convention.

In every case, Washington had acted out of a sense of duty rather than ambition, so it was with resignation that he finally set off on the long journey north to the new national capital and more responsibility. His trip became a personal triumph as every city and village along the way turned out to cheer the man already being called the "Father of His Country."

FIRST SENATE DEBATE

Washington arrived in New York on April 23, but his inauguration still was not immediately held. First Washington held a series of receptions for the new Congress. Of greater consequence, however, was that the U.S. Senate was engaged in its first great debate, that being the appropriate way to address the new president. Was he to be "His Majesty," "His Highness," or as one senator suggested, "His Most Benign Highness." John Adams worried about where, as presiding officer of the Senate, he should meet the president and where they should sit. He even worried about how to address the Speaker of the House, who would lead the representatives into the Senate chamber for the inaugural ceremony. Senator William Maclay of Pennsylvania noted dismissively in his diary that the Senate, particularly Adams, was obsessed with the "Goddess of Etiquette."

These questions of the rules of address were not as petty as they sound today. The heads of state that the new U.S. president would be dealing with were hereditary monarchs. There was no precedent for the title of an elected head of state.

Washington settled this question once and for all time. He made it clear that he would assume no title. To this day, the president of the United States is the only title given to the leader of our country, while members of Congress also assume the title "Honorable" and a judge is called "His Honor" or "Her Honor."

THE FIRST INAUGURATION

On the morning of April 30, both houses of the new legislature convened in the Senate chamber to witness Washington's inauguration. A dais had been set up at the Senate chamber window, which faced onto a balcony. This gave the citizens who filled the streets below a full view of the proceedings and the opportunity to witness the historic event.

As vice president of the United States and president of the Senate, John Adams was seated atop the dais. When Washington arrived, he was announced as the president of the United States. Adams stepped down from the dais and led Washington to this central seat, and then Adams took his own seat lower at the left. Similarly, the Speaker of the House, Frederick Muhlenberg, slipped into a lower seat at the right, thus ensuring that the leaders of both elected legislative bodies deferred to the president of the United States. These actions established precedents held to this day.

Such matters of etiquette seem quaint in our more casual society. Within the U.S. Congress, however, the restraints imposed by maintaining such formal behavior

George Washington is inaugurated as the first U.S. president at Federal Hall as Robert Livingston *(left),* chancellor of New York, administers the oath of office. The first debate in the Senate was over how Washington would be addressed, with one suggestion being "His Most Benign Highness." In the end, the only title for the leader of the United States would be president.

have enabled men and women to work together in spite of differing, even conflicting, opinions. This spirit of cooperation has led the nation forward, through times that none of those present at the first inauguration could have imagined.

To this day, the president still mounts the dais to address the Congress and is still announced to the chamber simply as: the president of the United States.

2

EQUAL REPRESENTATION FOR ALL

The Congress that met in 1789, consisting of the Senate and the House of Representatives, was not the first legislature in the United States. A system of representative government had been essential to the colonies since the arrival of the *Mayflower* in 1620, when its passengers signed the Mayflower Compact, the first governing document of Plymouth Colony. Representative governments continued with the state assemblies and Continental Congresses that carried these colonies to a national destiny.

Under the new Constitution, a two-chamber (or bicameral) legislative system now existed. All previous legislatures in the colonies, either within the individual colonies or loosely united as they had been since the Revolution, were single-chamber legislatures, just one group of male citizens selected to discuss and decide government matters.

A NEW SYSTEM OF CHECKS AND BALANCES

The delegates who met in 1787 at the Constitutional Convention in Philadelphia laid out a careful system of legislative checks and balances when they created the Constitution. They designed a system with a Senate, or upper house, in which members served six-year terms and were selected by their state legislatures, and a House of Representatives, in which members were elected by popular vote of the people every two years.

Each of the 13 original states would have two senators, giving small states like Delaware and Rhode Island equal voice with the larger states of Virginia, Pennsylvania, and Massachusetts. The decision to give states equal representation in the Senate was part of the Great Compromise, which grew out of two opposing ideas, the Virginia Plan and the New Jersey Plan. Under the Virginia Plan, the legislature would have two houses—membership in the lower house would be based on a state's population, and the lower house would elect the members of the upper house. The New Jersey Plan called for a one-chamber legislature in which each state would get an equal vote. The New Jersey Plan was also known as the Paterson Plan after William Paterson of New Jersey, the delegate

George Washington is shown presiding over a session of the Constitutional Convention in 1787 in Philadelphia. At the convention, the Great Compromise led to the creation of a bicameral legislature that addressed the concerns of both large states and small states. The formation of the Senate pleased the small states since it gave every state the same representation.

who worked to get the wishes of small states incorporated in the Constitution.

Paterson himself was born in Ireland. His family immigrated to America when he was a toddler. His father worked as a peddler on the American frontier but finally settled in New Jersey, where he founded a manufacturing business. Unlike his contemporaries George Washington, Thomas Jefferson, and even John Adams, Paterson did not come from an established or landed family, and he understood through his family's experience that the

Constitution needed to protect the rights of the least powerful as well as the interests of the majority.

Under the Constitution, the members of the House of Representatives assigned to each state would vary according to population. Representatives were originally apportioned one member to each 30,000 people in a state. This numerical equation has changed over time, but the principle of apportioning representatives based on population remains the same.

TERMS OF OFFICE

The Senate's terms of six years were staggered at two-year intervals, so that only one-third of the Senate is up for re-election in any election year. This idea ensures that a majority of senators at any given time have legislative experience. In contrast, the entire House membership serves two-year terms that expire simultaneously, meaning that the entire House is up for re-election every two years. With its membership changing at such short intervals, the House tends to be less bound to tradition than the Senate.

The first Senate included 22 members, while the first House of Representatives had 65 members—almost three times larger. The Senate, whose members were required to be at least 30 years old and were selected by their state legislatures, was considered the gentlemen's chamber. The proceedings of the Senate, in which elegant manners and refined speech mattered, were held in private. Meanwhile, the far more lively House of Representatives held its proceedings in public and even welcomed the press. Early on, the House—with its younger membership (the minimum age was 25)—received more attention in the press and made more of an impact on public opinion and policy.

OPEN TO THE PUBLIC AND PRESS

James Madison, often called the "Father of the Constitution," was asked many years later why he chose to run for a seat in the House of Representatives rather than seek the seemingly more prestigious Senate seat from Virginia. According to *Profiles in Courage, Young Readers Edition,* Madison believed that "as a young man and desirous of increasing his reputation as a statesman he could not afford to accept a Senate seat as its debates had little effect on public opinion."

The so-called Upper House felt uneasy that the more accessible representatives captured all the public attention. In 1794, the Senate authorized public galleries to be open at the regular legislative sessions. Arguments continued, however, over who could or could not come into the Senate. Women were not permitted to attend because it was thought that the senators would speak at length to get their attention.

Now, of course, with television cameras in both chambers, it is not even necessary to sit in a gallery seat to follow legislative action.

CONSTITUTIONAL POWERS OF THE SENATE

Besides setting terms of office and age restrictions, the Constitution laid out the principal responsibilities of the Senate. Article I of the Constitution deals exclusively with the Congress of the United States. Some provisions apply to both houses of Congress, such as the stipulation that no senator or representative may be appointed to any other office of the U.S. government during his or her term of office. Others deal with shared or joint powers, like impeachment (removal of high-ranking government officials from office), in which the House has sole authority to

ADVICE AND CONSENT: GEORGE WASHINGTON SETS THE PRECEDENT

★ ★ ★ ★ ★

When the first Senate convened in 1789, none of the senators knew exactly how the constitutional powers assigned to them would work in practice. In fact, no constitution and no government of this sort existed. For example, Article II of the Constitution, which outlines the president's powers, states that he must seek the "advice and consent of the Senate" to make treaties and to appoint ambassadors, other public ministers and consuls, judges of the Supreme Court, and all other officers of the United States.

George Washington knew most of the 22 members of the first Senate, and he interpreted the clause to mean he should attend a Senate meeting and discuss the matter with the entire body. Where there might be a need for "much discussion," Washington was inclined to think that personal consultation was best.

In August 1789, Washington walked over to the Senate with General Henry Knox seeking the advice and consent of the Senate on a treaty being negotiated with Southern Indians. The treaty was read. Questions arose and some senators complained about being unable to hear because of carriage noise outside the building. Other senators worried that the treaty contained information about public trans-

impeach (or charge) while the Senate has the power to try the case.

The Constitution gives the Senate sole power to confirm presidential appointments and ratify treaties. Yet in Article I, Section 7, the House is given the sole right to originate all bills that raise revenue for the government. The writers of the Constitution believed they were ensuring

actions unknown to the Senate. Finally, the senators concluded that they needed more information in order to vote. Washington listened to the quarreling and objections with a look of "stern disapproval." When the Senate decided to delay action until a committee had reviewed the treaty, the president announced, "This defeats every purpose of my coming here."

Still, Washington agreed to postpone the vote for two days to allow the Senate committee to meet. When Washington returned to the Senate, he listened with obvious boredom to several hours of debate before the treaty was approved with only minor changes. Washington was heard to say as he left the Senate that he would be "damned if he ever went there again."

From that day forward, when Washington needed the advice and consent of the Senate, he sent written material. If clarification was needed, he delegated one of his cabinet officers or a military official. Today all matters requiring the advice and consent of the Senate are reviewed exactly the same way. If that first attempt had been more of a success, however, we might still be watching the president of the United States personally discussing his requests with the Senate.

Alito Confirmation	
Y = 58 N = 42	
Clinton (D)	N
Coburn (R)	Y
Cochran (R)	Y
Coleman (R)	Y
Collins (R)	Y
Conrad (D)	Y
Cornyn (R)	Y
Craig (R)	Y
Crapo (R)	Y
Dayton (D)	N

YEA 58 NAY 42

Nomination of Samuel A. Alito, Jr., of New Jersey, to be an Associate Justice of the Supreme Court of the United States

One power that the Constitution gave only to the Senate was the confirmation of presidential appointments. Here, the vote is shown on January 31, 2006, after the U.S. Senate confirmed the nomination of Samuel Alito, Jr., to serve as a justice on the U.S. Supreme Court.

that weighty matters involving important offices and international agreements would be considered by the more thoughtful gentlemen of the Senate and that the younger men of the House would be more inclined to protect ordinary people in financial matters. As it turned out, since both the House and Senate must pass legislation, including revenue bills, for it to become law, this proved to be one more effective check and balance within the system.

Article I, Section 8 lays out a long list of congressional powers, including the power to tax, regulate commerce, establish uniform naturalization laws, coin money, and establish courts inferior to the Supreme Court as well as to raise and support armies and declare war. Congress did not get total power, however. For example, the president may veto bills passed in Congress, although Congress may override vetoes. Still, with the first Congress, it was a unique moment in the world when ordinary citizens assumed authority for the most powerful functions of government.

3

THE SENATE ORGANIZES ITSELF

The Senate immediately got down to business during its first session. No sooner had Washington been inaugurated than James Madison pushed the Congress to accept constitutional amendments to protect citizens' rights against intrusions from government.

Leaders in Rhode Island and North Carolina had refused to sign the Constitution because they did not believe that individual rights were sufficiently guaranteed under this new government. Therefore, one of the first actions of the Senate and the House was to pass constitutional amendments guaranteeing individual rights, including free speech and the right of assembly.

The House, where Madison served and led the debate, passed 17 amendments. These amendments were sent to the Senate, which reduced the number to 12. Eventually, 10 were ratified by three-fourths of the states to form what we now call the Bill of Rights. In response, Rhode Island and North Carolina joined the Union, increasing the number of states to 13 and the number of senators to 26.

The Senate then established the first executive departments. With the Revolutionary War still fresh in everyone's minds, the Senate created the War, State and Treasury Departments, enabling the new government to organize military defense, establish formal relations with foreign governments, and issue currency.

COMMITTEE OF THE WHOLE

Each of these important actions was considered by the Senate meeting as a committee of the whole. This meant that all of the senators sat in the chamber discussing the issue while Vice President John Adams presided. When the Senate agreed on its position, a committee was formed to write up legislation. After the bill became law, the committee was disbanded.

As each new item of business came to the Senate, it continued to meet in this manner. Members often sat around the fireplace, some writing letters and reading newspapers as if they were simply stopping at a men's club.

This clublike decision-making process did not mean that all senators held the same political opinions. There were senators who favored a strong federal government, and they were called Federalists. Those senators who wanted states to control matters inside their own borders took the name Democratic-Republicans. The Senate, though, was not structured to reflect these different political views.

Federalists dominated the Senate until 1800, when the Democratic-Republicans had a Senate majority and their informal party leader, Thomas Jefferson, was elected president. This also was the year that the government moved

THE SENATE AS A SAUCER, COOLING DOWN CRISES

★ ★ ★ ★ ★

When the Constitutional Convention met in 1787, Thomas Jefferson was the minister to France. Thus, the author of the Declaration of Independence did not participate in creating the Constitution or assume any position in the new government taking shape in New York City.

President George Washington recognized the situation and, on September 26, 1789, nominated Jefferson, a fellow Virginian, to be the first secretary of state. Jefferson had left France that very day and did not learn of his nomination until he was back in the United States on November 25, 1789. Jefferson had qualms about the office, as well as about the new legislative process created at the Constitutional Convention. He delayed officially accepting the position until February 14, 1790.

While visiting Washington at Mount Vernon, Jefferson raised concerns about the new bicameral legislature. Jefferson himself had served in single-chamber legislative bodies, including the Virginia House of Burgesses and the Continental Congress. What was the rationale for two legislative bodies to produce one final result?

The president is said to have answered his old friend: "You yourself have proved the excellence of two houses this very moment."

"How is that?" Jefferson replied.

to its new permanent capital city, Washington, D.C., mid-way between the Northern and Southern states.

In 1802, the Senate admitted stenographers and note takers to the chamber, acknowledging the need to keep a record of its deliberations. The informal, conversational tone of the discussion changed as words and votes

"You have turned your hot tea from the cup into the saucer, to get it cool. Even so," Washington observed, "we pour legislation into the senatorial saucer to cool it."

This anecdote was repeated as recently as April 24, 2006, by Senator Robert C. Byrd of West Virginia in a speech before the Senate. Byrd is the longest-serving senator in U.S. history. He first arrived in Congress in 1953 as a representative. In 1958, he was elected to the Senate and has served ever since. He has no intention of retiring.

Byrd himself has been cooled within the Senate chamber. He arrived as a Southerner who had participated in the Ku Klux Klan as a young man, and he voted against the first historic civil-rights legislation. Over time, his regional prejudices softened and disappeared. As recently as 2004, he was awarded a 100 percent approval rating from the National Association for the Advancement of Colored People (NAACP), the oldest and most influential civil-rights organization.

In the Senate saucer, Byrd transformed himself from a Southern firebrand into the Senate's historian and wise older gentleman. It is characteristic of the Senate that the institution reveres its own, often old-fashioned, traditions. Byrd continually reminds his fellow senators of the heritage they represent.

became a permanent record available for Americans everywhere to read.

THE SENATE REVISES ITS ORGANIZATION

After the national crisis of the War of 1812, the gentlemanly Senate finally acknowledged its administrative shortcomings. The new Capitol building had been partially destroyed on August 24, 1814, when the British invaded Washington. When the Senate reconvened, it met temporarily in modest quarters at the Blodgett's Hotel. Congress had lost all of its paper records, including the 740 books collected to form a Congressional Library.

The system of appointing select committees to refine legislative proposals was growing unwieldy. The Senate was spending too much time electing the members of those special committees. So in December 1816, the Senate created 11 permanent standing committees: Foreign Relations, Finance, Commerce and Manufactures, Military Affairs, Militia, Naval Affairs, Public Lands, Claims, Judiciary, Post Offices and Post Roads, and Pensions. The business of the Senate became more ordered and its records were protected.

It was a better organized, more seasoned, more wary Senate that was at work in the first half of the nineteenth century. As it turned out, the Senate needed this stronger framework as it moved into a period during which it angrily debated—with senators even resorting to physical threats—the question of slavery, the only major problem left unresolved by the Constitution.

In 1820, one year after the Senate returned to a newly restored Capitol chamber, it embarked on a bitter debate over whether the new state of Missouri would be a free state or a slave state. The legal and moral authority to hold slaves became the dominant question facing the Senate for the next 40 years.

In an atmosphere where the very existence of the precarious Union was under assault, the Senate finally became the powerful debating forum of selfless statesmen envisioned by the Founding Fathers. This difficult period is still called the Golden Age of the Senate.

THE WHIGS

The Senate agreed to a compromise, suggested by Henry Clay of Kentucky, on the Missouri question. Missouri would be admitted as a slave state if Maine was admitted as a free state. In 1836 and 1837, Arkansas and Michigan were admitted using this uneasy formula. Florida and Iowa came in as a pair in 1845 and 1846.

Clay, John Calhoun of South Carolina, and Daniel Webster of Massachusetts represented widely different parts of the nation. Clay was considered a Westerner, Calhoun represented the Southern aristocracy, while Webster stood for New England, with all the honesty and stubbornness this implied. These men did not agree on how to resolve the issue of slavery, but they did want to preserve the Union. The entire nation hung on these great spokesmen's words, which were published in broadsides (single-sheet printed documents) and repeated in the streets.

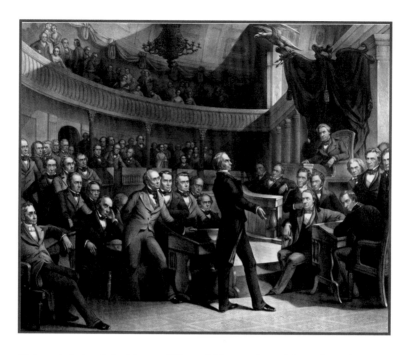

This print depicts Henry Clay of Kentucky addressing the U.S. Senate during a session in 1850. Senator Daniel Webster of Massachusetts is seated to the left of Clay, and Senator John Calhoun of South Carolina is seated to the left of the presiding officer's chair. With members like Clay, Webster, and Calhoun, the Senate became the powerful debating forum that the Founding Fathers had envisioned.

So powerful were these three senators that when they began to call themselves Whigs, this became the name of a new political party. (The name was chosen after the American Whigs of the 1770s, who fought for independence.) The Federalists had disappeared; only Democratic-Republicans still existed. Now two parties were restored to the Senate. Over time, political parties have shifted and new ones have emerged, yet the balance of a two-party system remains central to the legislative process.

In 1835, the Senate began to formally organize committees by assigning committee chairmanships to the ranking member of the majority party, which also controlled the majority of committee seats. From this point on, political parties determined the internal structure of the Senate.

A president pro tem, who would preside over the Senate in the absence of the vice president as authorized by the Constitution, had served since 1789. For many years, this position was filled on an as-needed basis when the vice president was sick or absent on business. The tradition has become that the Senate's longest-serving member in the majority party holds this position.

As the vice president's responsibilities grew within the executive branch, the president pro tem presided over more of the daily Senate business. In the 1950s, Vice President Richard Nixon physically moved the vice president's office out of the Capitol. Today, the busy president pro tem largely delegates the time-consuming assignment of presiding over the Senate to junior senators.

By the beginning of the twentieth century, the selection of majority and minority leaders at the beginning of each Congress by members of their own parties became the established practice. The majority leader is now regarded as the spokesman for the entire Senate, as the Speaker is for the House of Representatives. Today's Senate organizes its daily business through the majority leader's office. The minority leader ensures that the opposition party is represented.

The Whigs disappeared as a political party in 1852, fractured along anti-slavery and pro-slavery lines. The Civil War loomed on the horizon, and the Republican Party of Abraham Lincoln was germinating. What remains of the Whigs' legacy, though, is a politically structured Congress.

4

JOINT POWERS: IMPEACHMENT

The Senate and the House share equal authority over many congressional matters, including declaring war, maintaining the armed forces, and collecting taxes.

At first glance, one of Congress's joint powers seems to be more judicial and less concerned with the maintenance of the government as a whole. That power is the impeachment of a public official for wrongdoing. Impeachment, however, is not a criminal trial. The Senate is required to decide whether charges brought by the House of Representatives merit removing an official from office and disqualifying him or her from holding other offices and titles. If appropriate, the person may later be indicted, tried, and perhaps convicted and sentenced by judicial authorities, but none of these actions are imposed at the congressional level. Congress is simply empowered to decide whether the person should be removed from office.

Article I, Sections 2 and 3, of the Constitution discuss the procedure, and Article II, Section 4, indicates the grounds: "The president, vice president, and all civil officers of the United States shall be removed from office on impeachment for, and conviction of treason, bribery and other high crimes and misdemeanors."

The House of Representatives has the right to formally impeach (or charge) public officials for wrongdoing. It is the Senate, however, that hears the case against the official and votes for conviction. If the president of the United States is being tried, the chief justice of the Supreme Court must preside over the trial.

By the time of the Civil War, the House had impeached five top-ranking officials, including one U.S. senator, three District Court judges, and one Supreme Court justice. The Supreme Court justice and one of the judges were acquitted. The other two judges were found guilty and removed from office. The senator was expelled, and the charges were dismissed. There had not even been any suggestion of impeachment of either a president or a vice president.

The period that followed the Civil War, the bloody and bitter war between American brothers and cousins, was filled with strife. President Abraham Lincoln advocated moderate policies to restore the Union between the North and the South. Lincoln, though, was assassinated just a week after the Confederates surrendered at Appomattox Courthouse in Virginia. Andrew Johnson, the vice president, himself a

Andrew Johnson became president of the United States in 1865 after the assassination of Abraham Lincoln. Johnson had a cantankerous personality that put off many people. Almost immediately, he and Congress clashed over the Reconstruction of the South after the Civil War.

Southerner, vowed to continue Lincoln's post-war plan. A faction known as the Radical Republicans dominated Congress. These men sought a near military occupation of the

South, as well as the implementation of massive programs to assist the freed slaves. Their attitude was to use force rather than reconciliation to bring the Southern states back to the Union.

AN UNLIKELY PRESIDENT

Johnson was an unlikely president. In fact, he was an unlikely vice president. Like Lincoln, Johnson was born in a log cabin, in North Carolina. The son of illiterate parents, he was apprenticed at age 14 to a tailor by his mother and stepfather. After a couple of years, he returned to his mother, and the family moved to Greeneville, Tennessee, where Johnson set up a tailor shop.

He met and married Eliza McCardle, who educated her husband. By 1834, Johnson was a town alderman, and he later became the mayor of Greeneville. He identified with the common people and with rural problems. He went on to serve in the Tennessee state legislature and the United States House of Representatives before becoming the governor of Tennessee and then serving in the Senate.

Johnson was a senator when the Civil War broke out. He was the only Southern senator to retain his seat and continue in the U.S. Senate. He identified with Southern views on slavery but not on secession from the Union. Lincoln chose Johnson to be his running mate for his second term to balance the ticket and demonstrate that he was not controlled by abolitionists, the largely New England-based movement to end slavery.

This inspirational American story of a man rising from extremely modest beginnings ended with the indignity of being the first president of the United States to be impeached.

STANDOFF WITH CONGRESS

Although Johnson wanted to support Lincoln's humane measures toward the Southern states, he was less approving of the Freedmen's Bureau and other government-sponsored programs intended to ensure opportunity as well as freedom for the African-American population. Congress would send legislation to the president that he would veto,

The impeachment trial of President Andrew Johnson, which lasted nearly three months in the U.S. Senate, was a big draw in Washington, D.C. Shown above is a ticket for admission to the trial.

and then Congress would use its power to override the president's veto. This seesaw of legislation passed, vetoed, and then restored by Congress made an already difficult situation much worse.

It did not help that Johnson had a blustering, cantankerous personality that alienated people. His wife had taught him to read, but he never seemed to have learned the manners appropriate to the high offices he held. He was, as John F. Kennedy said, "courageous if untactful."

In 1867, the Radical Republicans finally enacted the Tenure of Office Act, overturning Johnson's veto. The act forbade the president from replacing federal officials without the Senate's consent. Specifically, Congress wanted to prevent the president from firing Secretary of War Edwin Stanton, who opposed Johnson's lenient policies in the South.

When Johnson discharged the secretary of war on February 21, 1868, Stanton refused to leave office, and Congress began impeachment proceedings based on the Tenure of Office Act. There were questions, however, about the constitutionality of the Tenure Act as it related to presidential appointments. A court of impeachment was constituted in the Senate on March 5, 1868, and Johnson's trial lasted nearly three months.

As it turned out, Johnson was acquitted by just one vote. The Senate at the time had 54 members and needed 36 votes, two-thirds of the members, to convict. All 12 Democratic senators and seven (of 42) Republicans voted against impeachment, which meant that Johnson remained

This drawing from the U.S. Senate Historical Society shows the impeachment proceedings against President Andrew Johnson. In the end, 35 of 54 senators voted to convict Johnson, one senator less than the required two-thirds majority.

in office because of one Republican vote. The seven Republicans who voted for acquittal all lost office in the next election. In 1887, the Tenure of Office Act was repealed, and in 1926 the Supreme Court ruled that a similar law was unconstitutional.

SUBSEQUENT PRESIDENTIAL IMPEACHMENTS

Only two other presidents have faced the possibility of impeachment. In 1974, President Richard Nixon resigned rather than face impeachment proceedings that were then being drawn up in the House of Representatives. Nixon faced possible charges of obstruction of justice, abuse of power, and contempt of Congress. These possible charges came in connection with the Watergate scandal, which occurred when men linked to the White House broke into Democratic Party headquarters at the Watergate Complex during the 1972 presidential campaign. Since many other top government officials were legally tried and sent

OTHER IMPEACHMENTS

The Senate's first impeachment trial came in 1798, and the proceeding involved one of its own members, Senator William Blount of Tennessee. The year before, the Senate expelled Blount, having found him guilty "of a high misdemeanor, entirely inconsistent with this public trust and duty as a senator." He was involved in a plot to incite Indians to assist the British in trying to conquer territory in Florida and Louisiana that was then under Spain's control. The impeachment proceedings against Blount, however, were dismissed since he no longer held office.

The first person impeached and found guilty was Judge John Pickering of New Hampshire. On March 12, 1804, the judge was found guilty of drunkenness and unlawful rulings. Many believed his mind had become unbalanced. A Harvard graduate, Pickering had a long, distinguished career serving in his state legislature and as a judge, culminating in his being named judge of the U.S. District Court in New Hampshire. He was removed from office after the guilty verdict and died one year later. His obituary stated, "Alas! The most brilliant talents are obscured when reason is dethroned."

The only Cabinet officer to be impeached was Secretary of War William Belknap, who served under President Ulysses S. Grant. A

to prison for their roles in the Watergate scandal, Nixon's decision was undoubtedly prudent. When Vice President Gerald Ford became president following Nixon's resignation, one of his first acts was to pardon Nixon.

President William Clinton, a Democrat, was impeached by the House of Representatives in December 1998 on

Union war hero who was a brigadier general under Grant during the Civil War, Belknap was wounded at Shiloh and participated in General William Tecumseh Sherman's Atlanta campaign and subsequent March to the Sea.

Belknap was accused of malfeasance in office for accepting more than $24,000 from a post trader who wanted to retain his position. Evidence showed that Belknap had received the payments from the post trader, but it was unclear if Belknap or his wife had made the arrangement or accepted the money. Just before the House was to vote on the articles of impeachment in 1876, Belknap resigned. The House, though, still sent the impeachment charges to the Senate. The Senate held a trial, but the vote to convict fell short of the two-thirds majority. He retired to a law practice and died in 1890.

Congress has generally used the impeachment process cautiously. An important precedent was established early when Associate Supreme Court Justice Samuel Chase, a strong Federalist, was impeached for judicial bias against anti-Federalists. Chase, though, was acquitted on March 1, 1805, in a decision that established that political differences were not grounds for impeachment.

charges of perjury and obstruction of justice. His impeachment stemmed from testimony he gave under oath about a personal relationship with a young woman. The impeachment trial in the Senate lasted from January 7 to February 12, 1999. The number of votes needed to remove Clinton from office was 67. The perjury charge was defeated with 45 votes for conviction and 55 against. The obstruction-of-justice charge was defeated with 50 for conviction and 50 against. No Democratic senators voted for conviction on either charge.

Impeachment is a powerful tool that allows the legislative branch to remove high-ranking officials from office for cause. Thanks to careful constitutional restrictions, though, the power has been cautiously used.

5

WHO MAY BE A SENATOR?

The Constitution states that a senator must be a citizen of the United States for at least nine years, be at least 30 years old, and be a resident of the state he or she represents. For more than a century, senators were chosen by their state legislatures, not directly by the voters. Both in law and in practice, this excluded many groups, not least of which were African Americans and women of any race.

The election of senators by the people was not required until the Seventeenth Amendment to the Constitution was ratified in 1913, one year before the election year of 1914. Until the middle of the nineteenth century, the system in which state legislatures selected senators worked efficiently, although it may have benefited special-interest groups in the states.

By the time of the Civil War, however, partisanship and discord over the question of slavery became so intense that some state legislatures were unable to elect a senator to represent them. In Indiana, the divisions between Democrats in Southern Indiana and the emerging Republican Party in the North were so bitter that the legislature had to leave a Senate seat vacant for two years.

After the Civil War, problems continued. There were 45 deadlocks in 20 states from 1891 to 1905. Delaware, for example, found its legislature so evenly split in 1899 that it did not send a senator to Congress for four years.

Oregon pioneered the direct election of senators, experimenting with various methods before finally instituting one that worked in 1907. By then, the direct election of senators was a popular reform issue throughout the United States, and the constitutional amendment was promptly ratified.

Long before senators were elected by popular vote, the question of who could serve was addressed.

AFRICAN-AMERICAN VOTING RIGHTS

After the Civil War in 1865, the Thirteenth Amendment abolished slavery, saying: "Neither slavery nor involuntary servitude . . . shall exist within the United States." The Fourteenth Amendment granted African Americans citizenship, and the Fifteenth Amendment stated boldly that "the right . . . to vote shall not be denied or abridged . . . on account of race, color or previous condition of servitude."

A political cartoon from 1870 shows Jefferson Davis, the former president of the Confederacy, looking over his shoulder as Hiram Rhoades Revels is seated in the U.S. Senate. The Mississippi legislature appointed Revels to fill the unexpired term of Davis's Senate seat, making him the first African-American senator.

Federal troops were sent to the South to protect the freedmen's rights, especially with regard to voting. Northerners assumed positions of authority over the defeated white populations. The Southerners despised their northern overlords for their arrogance and mistreatment of an already defeated people and called them "carpetbaggers" after the soft, fabric bags they used as quick-trip luggage.

THE FIRST AFRICAN-AMERICAN SENATORS

By 1870, the United States Senate had its first African-American senator, Republican Hiram Rhoades Revels of Mississippi. The state legislature had elected Revels to complete the unexpired term of Jefferson Davis, the former president of the Confederacy. Davis had vacated the seat almost 10 years earlier. Revels served one year, thus filling out what had remained of Davis's term.

In 1874, Blanche Kelso Bruce, also from Mississippi, was elected by the legislature, and he has the distinct honor of being the first African American to serve a full Senate term of six years. He was also the first to preside over the Senate. These early African-American senators were elected by state legislatures composed of African-American legislators, Yankee carpetbaggers, and what the white citizens thought of as riff-raff collaborators. These appointments left a bitter legacy in their wake, but given the opportunity to vote, the African-American population did so in record numbers, sending many African Americans into state legislatures and other elected offices.

Elected in 1874, Blanche Kelso Bruce of Mississippi was the first African American to serve a full term in the U.S. Senate. He was also the first to preside over the Senate.

As the federal troops and carpetbaggers pulled out of the South, the white population instituted voting requirements that effectively nullified the Fifteenth Amendment. These included literacy tests that kept many African Americans from exercising their voting right at a time when much of the population, both white and black, still legally signed their names with an X. In addition, Southern states instituted the poll tax, requiring people to pay to vote and shutting out blacks and poor whites.

These voting restrictions in the South did not change until the civil rights movement of the 1960s mobilized under Dr. Martin Luther King, Jr., who led a march on Washington, D.C., to demand protection of these constitutional rights. The legislative fight was bitter, but Congress did initiate and pass historic legislation in 1963 and 1964 to protect voting rights. These events effectively restored the voting franchise to African-American citizens.

After Reconstruction, no African-American senator was elected for almost 100 years. In 1966, Edward Brooke of Massachusetts became the first African American to be elected to the Senate by popular vote. He served with distinction for two full terms. Carol Moseley-Braun of Illinois became the first African-American woman senator with her election in 1992. Although she lost re-election in 1998, this enterprising woman became the U.S. ambassador to New Zealand. She raised the bar even higher in 2004 when she ran for the Democratic nomination for president.

The twenty-first century began more promisingly with the election of Barack Obama of Illinois to the Senate in 2004. Educated at Columbia University and Harvard Law School, where he became the first African-American president of the Harvard Law Review, Obama has made it a personal mission to focus on legislation to assist working families. He was elected an Illinois state senator in 1996, and during his run for the U.S. Senate seat in 2004, he gained national prominence when he delivered the keynote address at the Democratic National Convention.

WOMEN'S VOTING RIGHTS

The women's suffrage movement began seriously in the 1840s, and received its biggest boost when Susan B. Anthony joined the fight at the women's rights convention in

Syracuse, New York, in 1852 with her fierce commitment to the cause. During the period when the Reconstruction amendments were under discussion, suffragists urged language that would establish "universal suffrage," but they failed to attract sufficient support for women's suffrage.

In 1875, the Supreme Court heard the case of *Minor v. Happersett* and unanimously rejected the argument that

Fourteen women senators served in the 108th and 109th Congresses. They were *(seated from left)* Olympia Snowe, Blanche Lincoln, Barbara Boxer, Susan Collins, Dianne Feinstein, and Maria Cantwell, and *(standing from left)* Mary Landrieu, Hillary Clinton, Elizabeth Dole, Kay Bailey Hutchison, Barbara Mikulski, Lisa Murkowski, Deborah Stabenow, and Patty Murray. All 14 women continue to serve in the 110th Congress and have been joined by Amy Klobuchar and Claire McCaskill.

either the privileges and immunities clause or the equal protection clause of the Fourteenth Amendment could be used to extend the vote to women. For the next 41 years, a constitutional amendment to extend the vote to women was introduced in *every* session of Congress.

Some states and territories granted voting rights to women, the Territory of Wyoming being the first in 1869, and later Utah, Colorado, and Idaho. But it was not until 1920 that the Nineteenth Amendment passed. The amendment states, "The right of citizens of the United

MARGARET CHASE SMITH

★ ★ ★ ★ ★

No woman has served as long in the U.S. Senate as Margaret Chase Smith of Maine, who was a senator for 24 years. She also holds the distinction of being the first woman elected to the House of Representatives *and* the U.S. Senate. She won a special election to the House in 1940 to fill the vacancy caused by the death of her husband, Clyde H. Smith, a Republican congressman. She won re-election to the House four times.

In 1948, Smith ran for the U.S. Senate. In the primary, she initially had less funding and less name recognition than her opponents, and many questioned whether a woman should serve in the Senate. She overcame those odds, and in the primary, she won twice as many votes as her opponents combined. Smith went on to defeat her Democratic opponent in the general election by an overwhelming margin.

She gained national prominence in 1950, when she gave a speech on the Senate floor denouncing the tactics of Senator Joseph McCarthy's anti-communism campaign. During her time in the Senate,

States to vote shall not be denied or abridged by the United States or by any state on account of sex."

THE FIRST WOMAN SENATOR

The first woman senator, Rebecca Latimer Felton of Georgia, was appointed to fill out the term of her husband, Senator William Harrell Felton, who died in office. She was sworn in on November 21, 1922, and served exactly one day, the exact amount of time left of her husband's term.

Smith achieved a position of power, most notably as the ranking Republican member on the Armed Services Committee. She was also the ranking Republican member on the Aeronautic and Space Sciences Committee.

In her re-election to the Senate in 1960, Smith defeated Lucia Cormier; the race was the first in which two women opposed each other for a Senate seat. A few years later, Smith declared her candidacy for the 1964 Republican nomination for president, becoming the first woman to actively seek the presidential nomination of a major party. Her campaign was unsuccessful; Barry Goldwater was the Republican nominee that year.

Smith was defeated in 1972 in her bid for a fifth term in the Senate. It was the only race she ever lost in Maine. She received the Presidential Medal of Freedom in 1989 from President George H.W. Bush. Smith died in 1995 at age 97.

The next woman senator won election in her own right. Hattie Wyatt Caraway of Arkansas was elected to the Senate in 1932 and served until 1945. Thirty-one women have followed Caraway to the Senate. Maine and Louisiana have elected three women to the Senate. No woman to date has served as long as Margaret Chase Smith, who was a U.S. senator for four terms after winning election in 1948.

A record-high number of 16 women are serving in the Senate during the 110th Congress. They are Lisa Murkowski, Republican of Alaska; Blanche Lincoln, Democrat of Arkansas; Barbara Boxer and Dianne Feinstein, both Democrats of California; Mary Landrieu, Democrat of Louisiana; Susan Collins and Olympia Snowe, both Republicans of Maine; Barbara Mikulski, Democrat of Maryland; Deborah Stabenow, Democrat of Michigan; Amy Klobuchar, Democrat of Minnesota; Claire McCaskill, Democrat of Missouri; Elizabeth Dole, Republican of North Carolina; Hillary Clinton, Democrat of New York; Kay Bailey Hutchison, Republican of Texas; and Patty Murray and Maria Cantwell, both Democrats of Washington.

Of this distinguished group of women, Senator Hillary Clinton brings another first to her service, as the only first lady of the United States to serve subsequently as a U.S. senator. Still it is 87-year-old Rebecca Latimer Felton who earned the title of the first woman senator.

6

WHAT DOES A SENATOR DO?

The primary responsibility of a United States senator is to create, review, and vote on the legislation that governs our nation. The current Senate, with its 100 members, is a much different institution than the one that originally met in New York City. Now a single committee may have more members than the 22 men who made up the entire first Senate.

Instead of a committee of the whole sitting around informally discussing matters, present-day senators are assigned to serve on three or more of the 16 standing committees, four special and select committees, as well as joint committees that exist primarily for housekeeping and oversight. The legislation that is sent to these committees is their primary responsibility. Senators often introduce legislation of their own that may be sent to a committee on which they do not serve, but they will be called upon to provide supporting documentation and testimony to demonstrate why the legislation is needed.

The standing committees of the Senate are Agriculture, Nutrition, and Forestry; Appropriations; Armed Services; Banking, Housing, and Urban Affairs; Budget; Commerce, Science, and Transportation; Energy and Natural Resources; Environment and Public Works; Finance; Foreign Relations; Health, Education, Labor, and Pensions; Homeland Security and Governmental Affairs; Judiciary; Rules and Administration; Small Business and Entrepreneurship; and Veterans Affairs. The special and select committees are Indian Affairs; the Select Committee on Ethics; the Select Committee on Intelligence: and the Select Committee on Aging. The four joint committees, which have members from the Senate and the House of Representatives, are the Joint Committee on Printing; the Joint Committee on Taxation; the Joint Committee on the Library; and the Joint Economic Committee.

COMMITTEE OBLIGATIONS

Senators spend a significant amount of time studying legislative matters under consideration by their assigned committees. Most working days are largely related to committee work and do not involve debates in the Senate chamber. The senators have legislative staffs to follow the bills initiated by their particular committee assignments. Their staff members also keep the senators up to date on all legislative matters coming up for a vote on any given

Senator John Warner *(left)*, then the chairman of the Senate Armed Services Committee, and Senator John McCain, a member of the committee, met with reporters in September 2006 after a meeting on military tribunals. The bulk of a senator's day is devoted to committee work.

day, not just those involving one of their committees. In other words, the legislative staffs give the senators the information they need to develop their positions on issues and determine how they will vote.

The reason why the Senate chamber often looks so empty when C-SPAN televises its proceedings is that most senators are juggling several committee responsibilities on any given day. When a quorum (the number of senators required for a vote) is needed, bells ring in all Senate offices, committee rooms, and hallways. These bells mean that the senators have minutes to get to the Senate chamber and signify their presence. Staff members move quickly to make sure that their senator, who is leaving one area of responsibility, is fully informed on the pending vote. It is not unusual to see senators and their staff members deep in consultation while walking down office corridors or huddled in elevator corners.

If a senator must immediately return to the committee, he has the option of pairing, which means he records his vote with that of another absent senator, whose voting position is opposite. Thus an aye and a nay vote are recorded and cancel each other out, and the senator returns to his committee work.

DAILY OFFICE OBLIGATIONS

Each senator works in an office suite in one of three Senate office buildings—the Russell, the Dirksen, and the Hart office buildings. These are connected to one another as well as to the U.S. Capitol by underground passageways with small, open tram-cars that carry senators and staff members throughout the Capitol complex. This underground network connects to an identical tram-car subway system among the U.S. House of Representatives office buildings, which are also connected to the Capitol. It is an enclosed world. Each office building has cafeterias and snack bars (as does the Capitol), and the senators have a private dining room.

Each senator receives an allotment to hire staff and is assigned to an appropriate suite of offices. The salary funds that are provided depend upon the size of the senator's state and his or her seniority, as do the office arrangements. In general, this arrangement works well, since a senator like Hillary Clinton, who represents New York, obviously serves a large population and needs a larger staff allotment and more space. It is not uncommon, however, for a senator from a state with a small population to have enough of a national reputation and seniority that inevitably his staff allotment and office size become a problem, forcing the senator to turn to private funds or volunteers to augment the office arrangements.

At some place in the office suite, there will be a mail room or area, where hundreds of letters are sorted and acknowledged, while others are singled out for the senator's personal attention. Much of this mail still comes in written form, and some senators prefer that, but increasingly senators must take into consideration and respond to e-mail. Tabulating the results of Internet campaigns on particular issues has replaced the tallying of mass mailings that used to arrive by postcard.

A significant number of staff members, both in the Washington, D.C., and the state offices, are involved in constituent matters, which include everything from helping resolve a Social Security problem to securing tickets for a visitor to see the White House and even selecting young people for candidacy to the military academies.

On any given day, a senator will meet and talk with constituents, staff members, lobbyists, and fellow senators about matters before the Congress. The senator will return telephone calls and sign stacks of letters requiring his personal attention and signature. The letters that reach the senator's desk for signature are very important indeed, from personal friends or high government officials—matters for the senator's eyes only. However, a huge amount

A SENATOR'S DAY

★ ★ ★ ★ ★

On September 21, 2006, the U.S. Senate convened at 9:30 A.M. for morning business scheduled to last for 30 minutes. After morning business, the Senate resumed consideration of H.R 6061, the Secure Fence Act. There were no roll-call votes scheduled.

What really happened was that 13 measures were reported, including H.R. 6061, the Secure Fence Act, to establish operational control over the international land and maritime borders of the United States. The Senate voted unanimously to close further debate on this legislation and to proceed to consideration (the vote) of the bill.

Three confirmed nominations were announced, including Senator Barbara Boxer to be the representative of the United States to the Sixty-First General Assembly of the United Nations. Twelve nominations were reported as received and three as withdrawn.

Messages from the House were read, measures were referred to committee, and other measures were read for the first time. Executive reports were received from committees. Statements from senators on introduced bills and resolutions were submitted (most were submitted in writing for publication in the *Congressional Record*, which is distributed daily.)

The Senate adjourned at 6:42 P.M.

of the mail is processed and responded to routinely. Much of this mail is signed by automatic processes, but since these letters carry a senator's signature (even if not personally signed), no correspondence ever leaves the office until the senator has approved the language. This applies

On this typical Senate day, Senator Olympia Snowe of Maine:

• Attended the Committee on Commerce, Science and Transportation, which is one of her most important committee assignments. Her home state has vital transportation issues relating to its size, its long coastline, and interstate commerce.

• Joined fellow senators on the dais to participate in confirmation hearings for Mary Peters, nominated as secretary of transportation. Snowe used the occasion to ensure that Peters understood the importance of the Essential Air Service program to link rural Maine communities and to stress the importance of funding for transportation services like the Downeaster train service. Snowe met previously with Peters to discuss concerns, including truck weight limits and maintaining funding for Maine's four airports.

• Met with singer/songwriter Jewel, who came by in support of the Breast Cancer Patient Protection Act of 2005. Jewel and Lifetime Television delivered to Congress a petition with 12 million signatures in protest of what are called "drive-through" mastectomies. Later, Snowe met with 15 members of Maine's American Cancer Society Action Network. Both visits involved photographs and press releases.

• Was kept informed by staff members and other senators of every significant Senate action.

to e-mail responses as well—any information sent out under the senator's name must be approved.

With the legislative staff, the senator reviews the schedule of business before the Senate. His or her press secretary will request time to discuss language for press releases or press conferences. Inevitably, an important constituent from the home state will turn up in the reception area and be ushered in for a quick visit. Always there will be pressure to return to the home state, where the senator's presence is either requested or in some cases needed.

Each senator also has local offices that handle day-to-day matters back in the home state. These offices often take the lead in helping constituents who seek all kinds of assistance. Every day, the local offices (most senators have more than one office in their home state) and the Washington, D.C., office consult. The senator and staff give their local representatives information about national issues, which may raise questions that need to be addressed on the local level. Senators who represent states several time zones away often have one or more staff members who remain in the Washington office until all the state offices are closed.

IT NEVER ENDS

At the end of the day, it is a rare United States senator who heads directly home. There are receptions and political gatherings, and it is often prudent for the senator to make an appearance, at least briefly. These functions

Senators are called upon to return to their home states to tackle issues or work on problems there. Here, Peggy Fennelly *(left)*, owner of a candy shop in York Beach, Maine, points out flooded areas behind her store in May 2006 to Senator Olympia Snowe. With them was Charlie Summers of the Small Business Administration.

may include embassy receptions, events back home, or gatherings held by special-interest groups with ties to the senator's state. Sometimes the senator will send a staff member instead, so that no group feels overlooked. It would be physically impossible for senators to attend all these social events, many of which are important for political reasons. So senators pick among their options very carefully.

Finally there are the political chores. Depending on party affiliation, the senator is a member of either the Republican Caucus or the Democratic Caucus. These are private meetings for senators of one party during which they develop strategy on future votes and party matters. There also are conventions, speeches, and local political events deserving of attention. It is never safe to assume that any invitation or party gathering is unnecessary. For a senator, this whirlwind of activity ends only when he or she leaves office, which means either retirement or defeat.

7

CONSTITUENT SERVICES

Senators provide constituent services for all residents of their state. It does not matter if a person voted for the senator or how old someone is; senators have sworn to uphold the interests of their entire state population. To be sure, when it comes to legislative matters, the actions of senators will be shaped by the political party they represent, as will some of their appointments, but with constituent services all citizens are equal and anyone may call on senators and their staffs to provide these services. Members of the House of Representatives perform these same functions.

The range of Senate constituent services is wide. At the most basic level, senators through their offices can serve as intermediaries between constituents and the federal government. So if constituents have a problem or a question of eligibility involving the United States government that needs to be resolved or expedited or simply explained, they may turn to their senators for assistance.

This assistance is called casework. Governmental problems that a senator can help clarify or resolve range from mix-ups and confusion over Social Security benefits

PRIVATE LEGISLATION: 2006 WINTER OLYMPICS

Another way a senator may assist a constituent is by introducing private legislation. A private bill affects just one individual or organization, unlike public legislation, which governs everyone. Private bills are generally introduced when every other legal remedy has been tried. Most private bills involve complicated immigration problems, but other reasons include concerns over veterans' benefits, claims for a military decoration, or tax issues.

A private bill states, "For the relief of . . . ," indicating that it is intended for an individual. If a private bill is passed in one house of Congress, it must pass in identical form in the other house. These bills may not be amended or sent to conference committee.

In 1999, Canadian ice dancer Tanith Belbin of Quebec received her EB-1 visa after she came to the United States to train with her partner, Ben Agosto, in Michigan. This is an Extraordinary Ability visa extended to outstanding people in their fields, including executives and scientists as well as artists and athletes. Belbin began to train and compete with Agosto, receiving her immigrant worker visa in 2000 and her residency green card in July 2002, which meant Belbin could become a citizen in 2007.

to immigration difficulties to serious matters involving a Department of Veterans Affairs hospital. These cases are often of high importance, which is why the senator's office employs more than one caseworker to handle questions and problems from constituents.

Less dramatic, but no less necessary, the senator's office is available to help citizens learn what grants and

Belbin and Agosto hoped to represent the United States at the 2006 Winter Olympics, but the five-year waiting period seemed to stand in the way. They had already qualified to represent the United States in 2002 at the Olympics in Salt Lake City, Utah, but sat on the sidelines because Belbin was not yet a U.S. citizen.

In July 2002, U.S. Citizenship and Immigration Services changed the rules so that people could file for their immigrant worker and green card at the same time, thus speeding up the long process. If the rules had been in place when Belbin first applied, she would have had her citizenship in 2005.

Senator Carl Levin of Michigan said Belbin was caught in an administrative "catch-22," and he introduced legislation to allow the skater to qualify under current rules. The Levin Amendment S.A. 2268 passed the Senate and the House and was signed by President George W. Bush on December 31, 2005, the day that Belbin passed her citizenship test and became a U.S. citizen. The skaters went on to win the silver medal in ice dancing at the 2006 Olympics, the highest medal ever for a U.S. couple, and they were the first U.S. ice dancers to win an Olympic medal in 30 years.

federal assistance may be available to them, including educational and health-related support. In addition, state or local governments and their agencies often turn to the senator's office for advice on the best place to go in seeking assistance in such areas as disaster relief, homeland security, faith-based initiatives, and even consumer alerts.

Senators nominate candidates to the U.S. military academies. These include not only West Point, which officially is the U.S. Military Academy, but also the U.S. Naval Academy, the U.S. Air Force Academy, and the U.S. Merchant Marine Academy. The Senate office also distributes and answers questions about the application process. This responsibility is one that the senator and staff members take very seriously because these young men and women are the nation's future military leaders. The House of Representatives and the vice president of the United States can also nominate candidates.

The high school students who are selected to be Senate pages make up a very special group of Senate appointees. These high school juniors serve as messengers, still hand-carrying material around the Senate chamber and delivering papers at the request of senators. In addition, they distribute an agenda, copies of legislation, and any amendments to be voted upon to each desk in the chamber before the Senate is called into session. The students continue their high school education uninterrupted at the United States Senate Page School, although their real education occurs in this unusual close-up view of the Senate.

Aiming for the best angle, a visitor from Michigan takes a pic-
ture of the ceiling in Statuary Hall in the U.S. Capitol in December 2001. People who are planning to visit Washington,
D.C., can contact their senators' offices to arrange for tours
of various sites around the capital—just one of many constituent services provided by senators and their staffs.

The very first Senate page was appointed by Senator
Daniel Webster in 1829, and the House of Representatives began to use pages in 1842. The institution has en-
dured, and changed. Generally, senators with the most
seniority have the right to nominate a person to be a page,
but any senator may assist someone who inquires about
the program.

Until 1971, the pages were all young men, but in that
year, Senators Jacob Javits of New York and Charles Percy

of Illinois each appointed a young woman. Since then, the appointees have been both male and female.

Most senators offer an internship program for college-age students and recent graduates. The time spent working in the Senate office gives the participants an in-depth look at how the Senate actually functions. The students generally have arranged with their college or university to convert the experience into college credit. The postgraduate interns acquire valuable experience that will enhance their ability to seek a permanent job on Capitol Hill if that is their goal. The interns' salaries, if any, are minimal, but these positions are still greatly desired.

Senate offices also serve as something of a tourist bureau for visitors. By contacting their senators, people planning a trip may arrange for tours and tickets to visit all sorts of sites in Washington, D.C., from the White House to the Federal Bureau of Investigation. If visitors from the home state come to their senator's office, it isn't unusual for the senator to step out and say hello. Senator Lisa Murkowski of Alaska actually offers "Coffee With the Senator" on her Web site as an option that can be arranged before arriving in Washington, D.C.

One of the most interesting services that a senator offers to constituents is the opportunity to acquire an American flag that has flown over the United States Capitol. People may even request the particular date and time they wish the flag to fly. There are many reasons why people would want to receive a flag. Perhaps they wish to commemorate a historic occasion, or more personally, some event in their own family.

Employees of the Architect of the Capitol raise and lower
American flags on the roof of the U.S. Capitol in Washington,
D.C. Constituents may contact their senators to purchase a
flag that has been flown over the Capitol.

This service does mean that American flags go up the pole and then come down all day long. Every flag that goes out to a constituent has in fact flown over the Capitol and comes with verification of the exact time and date. This is one of the most popular services available, and a huge backlog of orders always exists. The cost to the constituents is small, depending upon whether they want a nylon or a cotton flag and what size they prefer. People who work or live on Capitol Hill soon become used to the sight of flags going up and then, soon after, coming down.

It is the senator's responsibility, and pleasure, to provide these constituent services. These are among the most powerful and human of the contacts between the people and their elected official. So although the bustle of legislative activity dominates the Senate calendar and the daily news, in actuality a substantial part of the staff in any senator's office is taking requests for tours of the Library of Congress, or checking up on a missing Social Security check, or looking into a grant program for a constituent. This is democracy in action.

8

SENATE OFFICERS AND STAFF

Thousands of people are employed within the three Senate office buildings and the U.S. Capitol to keep the Senate's complex and constantly shifting responsibilities on course. These employees fall into two groups, Senate officers and Senate staff. The officers are those people who serve the entire Senate, some but not all of them senators themselves. These people handle the administrative and managerial functions of the day-to-day operations of the Senate. Second are the senator's personal staff members, selected and hired by him or her, who work on the senator's behalf.

SENATE OFFICERS

The Constitution states that the president of the Senate shall be the vice president of the United States, who presides over the sessions but votes only in the case of a tie. For many years, that remained the vice president's chief responsibility, and his offices were in the U.S. Capitol. However, provisions had to be made for an officer who could preside in the vice president's absence, thus the Constitution provided a second presiding officer, the president pro tempore, also known as the president pro tem. At first this was a temporary appointment made only when it was known that the vice president would be absent or was ill, and sometimes more than one senator served as president pro tem during a session. In the early years, the president pro tem was elected on the basis of popularity and reliability. During the twentieth century, the present custom began of making the senior senator of the majority party the presiding officer.

Party secretaries, elected by both the majority and the minority parties, are employees who are seated at either side of the Senate chamber. Their day-to-day chores include making sure the pages are in place, scheduling legislation, and keeping senators informed about pending business in the session.

There also is a secretary of the Senate, whose office oversees a vast array of administrative functions. It disburses the payroll, acquires and distributes official stationery and cards, oversees the Page School, and maintains public records. The first secretary of the Senate was Samuel Otis, a close friend of Vice President John Adams's. He was elected on April 8, 1789, just as the Senate began to organize.

William Pickle, then the sergeant at arms of the U.S. Senate, is shown in his Capitol Hill office in 2004. The sergeant at arms serves as the chief law enforcement officer, protocol officer, and executive officer of the Senate.

The sergeant at arms and doorkeeper serves as the protocol officer, executive officer, and chief law enforcement officer of the Senate. The doorkeeper's major responsibility goes back to 1789, when the Senate had trouble getting the necessary number of members on the floor to open the first Senate session. The day after the first Senate finally achieved a quorum and could officially function, it locked the doors and elected its first doorkeeper. He was appointed to keep the members inside once the required majority was on hand. He also was responsible for ensuring order on the Senate floor and in the galleries.

In 1798, the title of sergeant at arms was added to that of doorkeeper.

As the chief law enforcement officer, the sergeant at arms can literally insist that senators come to the Senate chamber. The sergeant at arms also provides security within the U.S. Capitol and all the Senate office buildings and has the authority to detain anyone in violation of Senate rules, even the president of the United States.

As the Senate's chief protocol officer, the sergeant at arms coordinates all official occasions in the Senate. The sergeant at arms leads the president to the inaugural platform and leads senators into the House chamber for the State of the Union address. As the Senate's executive officer, the sergeant at arms enforces all the rules within the Senate chamber and in committees.

The sergeant at arms's office provides an enormous amount of administrative support to the Senate, including software, computers and equipment, and repairs to Senate offices. It prints everything from stationery to newsletters. Plus, every day it sorts and distributes the mail. It even builds Senate furniture.

No officer of the Senate is more vitally important than that of the legislative counsel, who is appointed by the president pro tem. The Office of the Legislative Counsel, which has existed since 1919, drafts legislation at the request of senators and committees. The office has a non-partisan staff that creates the appropriate legal language in which a proposal can be considered for passage into law.

There is also a Senate chaplain, another office that goes back to the first Senate, which elected the Right Reverend Samuel Provoost, Episcopal bishop of New York, to be its first chaplain on April 25, 1789. The office's responsibilities include opening the Senate each day with a prayer, holding discussion sessions, counseling senators, their families, and their staffs, as well as sponsoring a weekly Senators' Prayer Breakfast.

Senator Arlen Specter spoke to reporters in May 2006 after the Senate voted to overhaul the nation's immigration laws. With him were *(from left)* Harry Reid, then the Senate minority leader; Senator Edward Kennedy; and Bill Frist, then the Senate majority leader. The majority and minority leaders are the main floor leaders in the Senate.

Besides these officers of the Senate, two other positions hold great power. These are the floor leaders, or the majority leader and minority leader of the Senate. The majority

THE LOOK OF A SENATOR'S STAFF

★ ★ ★ ★ ★

Powerful senators who represent states with large populations, like Senator Arlen Specter of Pennsylvania, have huge staffs. Senator Specter was elected to the Senate in 1980. Pennsylvania is the sixth-largest state, with a population (according to the 2000 census) of 12,281,054. Representing such a large constituency gave the senator some influence from the beginning, but he has accumulated much more during his long stint of service.

In the 109th Congress, Specter was chairman of the Judiciary Committee, one of the most powerful Senate chairmanships. He was also senior member of the Appropriations Committee, another position of great authority, and chairman of the Appropriations Committee's Subcommittee on Labor, Health and Human Services, and Education.

Specter's staff reflects the magnitude of these responsibilities as well as the size of the state he represents. His Washington, D.C., staff lists 29 employees. Adding the 25 staff members who work in his seven offices in Pennsylvania, the total number of people he employs is 54. This does not include his staff members who work for the committees and subcommittees he serves on.

In Specter's Washington office, 11 employees carry administrative titles ranging from administrative director to staff assistant/receptionist. In this day of Internet communication, his systems administrator is of

leader and minority leader are elected by senators of their respective political parties—the majority leader being from the party that has the most senators. These leaders

key importance, as the senator maintains a sophisticated Web site and receives thousands of e-mails.

The greatest number of staff members devoted to one area work on legislative duties. The titles of the 13 employees range from legislative assistant to legislative aide and legislative correspondent. Each of these people is assigned to specific legislative areas. Only two people, a press secretary and a deputy press secretary, take care of the senator's press needs.

Four of the senator's field offices have caseworkers or constituent services representatives. All of the field offices are headed by an executive director. Only his large Philadelphia office employs a senior legislative assistant; Philadelphia is Specter's home town and the site of the state's most influential newspapers and television stations, so it is in his interest to keep someone familiar with current legislative matters at this office.

To put this in perspective, consider Senator Mike Enzi of Wyoming, whose state is dead last in population at a mere 493,782. At the same time, it is big in size, the eleventh-largest state. Having served since 1997, Senator Enzi had risen to become the chairman of the Senate Health, Education, Labor, and Pensions Committee in the 109th Congress. His Washington, D.C., staff consists of 18 people. With nine staff members working in five offices in Wyoming, his total staff is 27, or less than the number Specter has in only his Washington office.

serve as the chief Senate spokespersons for their parties, and they manage and schedule the legislative and executive business of the Senate.

A SENATOR'S STAFF

Each of the 100 senators has a personal staff that works in a suite of offices in one of the Senate office buildings. The senator's staff is hired by and for the senator personally to work on legislation, do casework, handle press relations, and fill clerical functions. The senator alone is responsible for these appointments. The senator's staff salary allotment and office suite are based on the size of population he represents as is his office suite. Senators with personal means sometimes augment their staff by paying for additional employees, and there are always people willing to work without salary as interns or volunteers in order to have the experience of being closely involved with the business of the nation.

One person in the office carries the title of chief of staff, or executive director, which indicates that he or she is in charge of the office. This is a position of high trust, of someone close to the senator, who has authority over all the units that make up the senatorial operation. A chief administrator ensures that day-to-day operations are staffed and executed. There is also someone who is the equivalent of what used to be called a personal secretary, who handles the schedule as well as the most personal matters.

A legislative director, with several assistants, is in charge of following the legislative schedule and ensuring that the senator is informed and advised about legislation active on the Senate floor. If the senator is a chairperson or ranking member of a committee, he or she will have staff members on the committee, who coordinates their work with the personal office. Casework is directed by one person, although several caseworkers are on staff.

Everything that happens in the senator's office is carried out in his or her name. The staff works behind the scenes, and most visitors are surprised at the size and complexity of actual Senate offices. It is important that the staff members remember that they are there to serve the interests of the senator and the state he or she represents.

9

How a Bill
Becomes a Law

If a senator is interested in sponsoring a bill, which means taking a lead position in getting the legislation passed, he asks his staff to submit the bill proposal to the office of the Senate's legislative counsel. This office will put the proposal into appropriate legal language. At the same time, senators and staff members begin to accumulate background information from the Congressional Research Service at the Library of Congress, financial information from the Government Accountability Office (formerly the General Accounting Office) and the Congressional Budget Office, as well as any other technical feasibility background that may be required.

Once the research is completed and the senator and the staff are satisfied with the legislative counsel's draft, the senator begins to look for co-sponsors among his colleagues. The proposed legislation will be circulated among all the senators, regardless of party. The senator hopes to find a co-sponsor from the opposing political party. Bipartisan support makes the bill stronger since both parties are represented at the top of the legislation. Additionally, the senator hopes to secure a large number of other sponsors.

THE BILL IS INTRODUCED

When the co-sponsors have been secured, the senator takes the bill to the Senate chamber, where he formally introduces it. Not many people will be present at this occasion, which is purely administrative. The introduction of the bill and any supporting statements submitted by co-sponsors will be placed in the *Congressional Record*, which will reach every congressional office the next day.

The legislative clerk assigns a number to the bill. A Senate bill numbered S. 238 indicates that it is the 238th Senate bill introduced in that session of Congress. Senior senators can reserve an enrollment number (a favorite being 1776) to give their legislation an easy way to get attention. The parliamentarian refers the bill to the appropriate committee, which sends it to a specialized subcommittee.

Once the bill has a committee assignment, its journey to becoming a law has begun. The first hurdle the bill must surmount is subcommittee approval. The subcommittee may decide to hold hearings if the matter is complex or calls for public discussion. After the hearings, the

Committee hearings are not necessarily staid meetings filled with speeches and statistics. Here, a demonstrator is led from a Senate Foreign Relations Committee hearing in July 2006. The committee was holding a hearing on the permanent nomination of John Bolton to be United Nations ambassador.

subcommittee meets not to vote on the bill but to decide whether to send it to the full committee.

If it gets to the full committee, the bill enters into the process of being "marked up," which simply means that every word in it is reviewed, and revisions are made where confusion may occur or the intent is unclear. Pressure is applied daily from lobbyists, official and unofficial, who want to see the bill voted out of committee. Senators who oppose the version of the bill that they anticipate will come out of committee may introduce legislation representing their own position.

The bill's sponsors work to get support, talking with the press, making speeches, building alliances within the Senate, and even promising to support another senator's bill in return. The public is asked to indicate its support with letters, e-mails, and phone calls.

THE FULL COMMITTEE REPORTS

When a committee reports on a bill, it either votes to send it to the Senate for confirmation or to kill it. If the bill seems likely to pass, the reporting senator can ask for unanimous consent, and if this is secured, the bill goes to the Senate without change. Opponents, though, can put a hold on the legislation to make changes, including adding amendments.

If unanimous consent cannot be reached, then the full Senate debates the matter. The committee chairman, subcommittee chairman, or sponsor becomes the floor manager, the person designated to lead and organize consideration of the bill, and one of the opponents becomes the opposition manager. These two senators must speak before the whole Senate can debate the legislation.

Now the debate turns into a strategic matter. Opponents may use the filibuster, which means talking indefinitely to prevent a vote on the bill. They can introduce more amendments from the floor. Further, they can constantly interrupt Senate business by requesting quorum calls to bring the required number of senators to the floor. A filibuster can be overcome through cloture, under which the Senate can vote to place a time limit on the consideration of a bill. Three-fifths of the Senate, or 60 senators, must vote to approve cloture.

If the bill passes the Senate, it is sent to the House of Representatives, where it goes through a similar process. If it passes the House, the bill still must go to a conference

GOOGLE FOR GOVERNMENT

On September 26, 2006, Senator Barack Obama exulted, "I finally got a bill passed." With less than two years in the Senate, he had a right to be excited. Legislation can take years to become law. For S. 2590, Obama was joined as chief co-sponsor by Senators Tom Coburn of Oklahoma, John McCain of Arizona, and Tom Carper of Delaware. Obama and Carper are Democrats, while Coburn and McCain are Republicans.

S. 2590 states that it is "a bill to require full disclosure of all entities and organizations receiving federal funds." Basically its implementation would allow any American citizen with Internet access to see exactly where federal tax dollars are being spent. The bill covered everything from block grants to indirect financial assistance.

Specifically, the legislation was intended to eliminate "earmarks," which are last-minute or privileged additions to spending bills that benefit specific senators or states. This unsavory custom is also called "pork barreling," because the senator is rolling home the bacon. Earlier the House had passed a similar bill.

There was widespread support for this piece of open-government legislation, which coincided with an election year. It was introduced in the Senate on April 6, 2006, and sent to the Senate Homeland Security and Government Affairs Committee, which handed it over

committee of the Senate and House because it is unlikely that the House passed a bill that did not include amendments of its own. The conference committee must find a way to reconcile any differences between the bill passed in the Senate and the one approved in the House. If no

to its Subcommittee on Federal Financial Management, Government Information, and International Security.

On July 27, 2006, the full committee approved the bill unanimously, and it was placed on the Senate calendar for August 2. Then two holds were placed on the bill. Holds are an entirely legal Senate privilege exercised when a senator wishes to ensure that the legislation does not immediately come up for a vote. Once a hold is in place, no action can be taken until it is withdrawn.

Bloggers went into action after hearing news of the secret holds impeding the legislation. The Senate was besieged with outraged e-mail. Bloggers discovered that Senators Ted Stevens (the president pro tem) and Robert Byrd had placed the holds. Both gentlemen are famous for delivering funds to their home states. Senate Majority Leader Bill Frist announced that he would bring the legislation to the floor, holds or no holds. As the furor increased, both senators found it politic to withdraw their holds.

On September 7, the bill passed unanimously and went to the House of Representatives, where differences were settled and the bill passed. President George W. Bush signed it into law on September 26. Senator Obama celebrated, saying, "Now people can Google for government."

consensus is reached, the legislation dies. If changes are made that satisfy both the Senate and House conference committee members, the bill is returned to both chambers for a vote.

At this point, if the Senate and the House of Representatives approve the bill as presented by the conference committee, it is considered passed and is sent to the White House. The bill is still not ready to become law. The president can approve and sign the bill into law, or he can veto it, or he can do nothing. If he does nothing, the

Senator Norm Coleman, a Republican from Minnesota, spoke in November 2003 during the thirty-fourth hour of a marathon session organized by Republicans to protest Democratic filibusters. Filibusters are used to prevent a vote on a bill. Coleman was discussing the judicial nomination of Charles Pickering, which had been blocked by a Democratic filibuster.

bill becomes law in 10 days. If Congress adjourns before the 10 days are up, the president need not take any action. The bill will simply die in his "pocket," the so-called pocket veto. If he vetoes the bill, a two-thirds majority of both houses need to override the veto for the bill to become law.

There is nothing easy about making a law, which is as it should be.

10

PAST AND
PRESENT

If John Adams were to walk into today's Senate chamber, there would be many aspects that startle him. He would certainly be surprised by the size of the Senate, with 100 members, and dismayed by the television cameras. The names of both political parties would mean nothing to him, and he would not be too comfortable with the dominance of the parties or with the amount of animosity occasionally generated between them.

Undoubtedly the protocol-conscious Mr. Adams would be horrified at a voting procedure that allows senators at least 15 minutes to stroll over to the Capitol and register their vote. Worse, from his point of view, he would find few if any senators sitting in the chamber discussing legislative matters. In fact, he would be lucky if he found anyone present during the session other than the presiding officer, who would not be, as in the days of John Adams, the vice president of the United States. Most likely, a very junior senator would be filling that parliamentary function.

The legislative clerk probably would be present, although Adams would have no idea of the clerk's function in recording votes in the twenty-first century. The clerk records votes as senators approach the desk; senators do not vote at their seats as was the custom in Adams's day. Most senators immediately leave to return to responsibilities elsewhere. Adams certainly would miss the high drama of having each vote called out from the senators at their desks, a sight he would only see if he arrived at a time of high crisis requiring something like a declaration of war.

He would see young adults in uniforms, male and female, carrying messages and putting material on the senators' desks. If he asked, he would be told that these young people were Senate pages, teenagers in their junior year of high school who are appointed by senators to their positions. Having a person, even a young one, carry messages among the senators, however, would seem quite proper to Adams, although he would have to adjust to the senators being called away to a telephone call or rushing out in the hall to answer a cell phone. It's hard to imagine what Adams would think of the young women pages—or of women serving as senators. Undoubtedly his intelligent wife, Abigail, would think both were long overdue.

He would be astonished at the range of responsibilities that senators have in the twenty-first century. Although he would be reassured that the Senate was still the upper chamber, with its reputation as the more deliberative body remaining intact, he would be amazed that modern senators can take as much time as they do to reflect on serious matters. In Adams's day, no senator was running an office in which staff members were trying to resolve constituent problems or arrange a White House tour. In

ANTIQUE DESKS AND E-MAIL

The Senate respects its own traditions. It still uses language and furniture that would not be unfamiliar to the first Senate in 1789, and it continues customs, like providing snuff boxes, that have no place in the twenty-first century. This sense of continuity and respect for tradition gives the Senate a special quality. Senators with longer terms of service are encouraged in this atmosphere to become the statesmen, rather than politicians, that the Founding Fathers intended of the upper house.

Since the late nineteenth century, Democrats sit to the left of the chamber aisle facing the presiding officer. On the right side of the aisle, Republicans traditionally take their seats. Desks are moved across the aisle when one party increases its membership. Senators pick their desks at the start of each new session in order of seniority. Reasons for selection range from how close the desk is to an exit door to whether the desk is in a good position for the television cameras.

Tradition plays a part, too. The senior senator from New Hampshire sits in what is known as Daniel Webster's desk. Webster represented Massachusetts in the Senate, but he was born in New Hampshire. The desk of Jefferson Davis, who left his Senate seat at the beginning

fact, in Adams's time, only a senator with personal means could afford to keep a personal secretary (always a man) to assist him.

MR. ADAMS WOULD BE PLEASED

Adams, though, would feel reassured that senators still formally addressed one another during debates as "the

of the Civil War to become president of the Confederate States, is always occupied by the senior senator from Mississippi. Senator Edward Kennedy of Massachusetts was given the desk of his brother, former Senator and President John F. Kennedy.

Many of these desks date to 1819, when they replaced ones burned by the British during the War of 1812. As the Senate expanded, new desks were built to match the old ones. Since much of a senator's actual work takes place elsewhere, a more functional desk is unnecessary for the Senate chamber. The elegant old desks are perfectly sufficient to hold the daily agenda and materials distributed by the pages, as well as any notes or prepared speeches a senator may need.

Back in the senator's bustling office, staff members will be checking e-mail messages. The communications people will be noting e-mail campaigns on behalf of a particular issue. The press people may be putting together the senator's Internet newsletter, while others are checking the constituent requests sent through e-mail. Meanwhile, over on the Senate floor, the senator is possibly leaning on his nineteenth-century desk talking with a colleague across the aisle.

During a photo session in the old Senate chamber, Senator Max Cleland gave the "Scoop" Jackson desk in 2001 to
a newly sworn-in senator, Maria Cantwell of Washington.
Cleland had used the desk for the previous four years. It was
once used by Henry "Scoop" Jackson, a legendary senator
from Washington. Many of the desks in the Senate chamber
date from 1819.

Honorable Gentleman from . . ." He would also feel at ease with the good manners and collegiality that still exists across political differences in the Senate.

The process of how a bill becomes a law remains basically the same. A bill is passed by the Senate, sent to the House, and then differences are resolved in a conference committee before the president signs the proposal into law. He would, however, be overwhelmed by the magnitude of the process in the twenty-first century. The Senate has many committees and subcommittees, each functioning in ways John Adams could not have imagined in the eighteenth century. Back then, the entire Senate met together and talked casually about what a particular bill should say, and then several senators were asked to write up the proposal. The idea that a committee would consider all the pros and cons of legislation, and much of the work would be done by paid staff, and this committee would make recommendations to the Senate would be very difficult for an eighteenth-century gentleman to understand. As for the "Google for government" bill, the idea of the public petitioning Congress over cyberspace would probably make John Adams feel as if he had landed on the moon.

He would like the quiet, elegant look of the Senate chamber with its horseshoe of simple knee-hole desks, even the newest made to match the 1819 version that replaced the desks burned by the British in 1814. He would not be surprised to find snuff boxes in the Senate, although most new senators are. However, he would wonder why the one large snuff urn under the presiding officer's rostrum had been replaced with two small ones, on each side of the rostrum. This would seem to be especially puzzling because no one uses the snuff. In Adams's day, senators had crowded at the base of the presiding officer's rostrum to jostle for snuff, a form of tobacco that is either chewed or inhaled. The change to two boxes on either side of the chamber came in an attempt to stop the crowding and noise where the presiding officer was trying to conduct business. It has been years since anyone used snuff, but such is the seriousness with which the Senate takes its traditions that the two small boxes still are in place.

Surely he would be amused that instead of snuff, senators make a quick stop at the desk in the back row of the Republican side of the Senate on the aisle nearest the side door, the so-called Candy Desk. By tradition, the senator at this desk keeps a bowl of hard candy handy for colleagues to grab as they enter the chamber. These senators usually complain, and often get help with the expense, but they continue the tradition.

Yet the biggest surprise would surely be that, almost 225 years later, the Senate's responsibilities remain exactly as set out in the Constitution. How proud this eighteenth-century gentleman and second president would be to see that the Founding Fathers' work had been solid enough to stand unchanged in the twenty-first century, even if some of the furnishings might be different.

GLOSSARY

amendment An addition or a change to a bill or a document.

bicameral Two separate bodies that combine to make one whole.

bipartisan Of, relating to, or involving members of two parties; specifically, marked by or involving cooperation, agreement, and compromise between two major political parties.

cloture Three-fifths of the Senate voting to stop a filibuster.

compromise An agreement in which all sides concede some advantage in the interest of achieving a larger goal.

constituent A resident of the state that a senator represents in the U.S. Congress.

filibuster A tactic used in the Senate to delay or prevent a vote by making a long or continuous speech.

impeachment The House of Representatives may bring a charge of impeachment (removal from office) against the president, the vice president, and other top-ranking officials on charges of bribery, treason, or other serious misconduct. The Senate hears the charge. If it votes for impeachment, the official is removed from office.

lobbyist An individual, or an organization, who represents a special-interest group, an industry, or a political goal, and who tries to use facts and influence to gain votes for the interests he or she represents. In early times, they lingered in the Senate lobby.

nonpartisan Free from party affiliation, bias, or designation.

president pro tempore A senator elected to preside when the president of the Senate (vice president of the United States) is absent.

quorum The minimum number of senators who have to be present to conduct business. In today's Senate, a quorum is 51 members—one-half the membership of 100 plus one.

ratify To accept, approve, or endorse, particularly important in the Senate, which has the constitutional authority to ratify U.S. treaties.

repeal To take back or to cancel. In a legislative sense, it would mean to cancel a former act.

standing committee A permanent committee of the Senate with continuing authority over legislation in one major area.

suffrage The right to vote.

veto The power of the president to refuse to sign a bill passed by Congress; the bill is prevented from becoming law unless it is passed again with a two-thirds majority by both houses of Congress.

BIBLIOGRAPHY

Bansfield, Susan. *James Madison*. New York: Franklin Watts, 1986.

Banks, Joan. *The U.S. Constitution*. Philadelphia: Chelsea House Publishers, 2001.

Ferris, Robert G. & Robert H. Charleton. *The Signers of the Constitution*. Flagstaff, Arizona: Interpretive Publications, 1986, reprinted from the National Park Service, 1976.

Hoopes, Roy. *What a United States Senator Does*. New York: John Day Co., 1970, revised ed. 1975.

Kennedy, John F. *Profiles in Courage, Young Readers Edition, abridged*. New York: Harper & Row, 1955; Young Reader's Edition, 1961.

Phelan, Mary Kay. *The Burning of Washington 1814*. New York: Thomas Crowell Co., 1975.

Quackenbush, Robert. *James Madison and Dolley Madison and Their Times*, New York: Pippin Press, 1992.

Ritchie, Donald. *The Senate*. Philadelphia: Chelsea House Publishers, 1988.

Ritchie, Donald. *The Young Oxford Companion to the Congress of the United States*. New York: Oxford University Press, 1993.

Web Sites

National Constitution Center
www.constitutioncenter.org

U.S. Senate

www.senate.gov

U.S. State Department's Basic Readings in U.S. Democracy:

http://usinfo.state.gov/usa/infousa/facts/democrac/demo.htm

FURTHER READING

Dewhirst, Robert. *Encyclopedia of the United States Congress.* New York: Facts on File, 2006

Hamilton, Lee H. *How Congress Works and Why You Should Care.* Bloomington, Ind.: Indiana University Press, 2004.

Ritchie, Donald A. *The Congress of the United States: A Student Companion.* New York: Oxford University Press USA, 2001.

Web Sites

Ben's Guide to U.S. Government for Kids
http://bensguide.gpo.gov/

FirstGov for Kids
www.kids.gov

The National Archives Experience: Constitution of the United States
www.archives.gov/national-archives-experience/charters/constitution.html

Thomas: The Library of Congress (legislative information from the Library of Congress)
http://thomas.loc.gov/

The United States Capitol Historical Society
www.uschs.org

PICTURE CREDITS

INDEX

ABOUT THE AUTHOR

JANET ANDERSON has written hundreds of newspaper and magazine features, as well as theater and dance reviews, for publications like the *Los Angeles Herald Examiner, Philadelphia Inquirer, Philadelphia Daily News, City Paper* of Philadelphia, and *Playbill*. She has written one other book for Chelsea House Publishers. Anderson also worked at the United States Congress, for much of the time as a legislative aide on the staff of Senator Mark O. Hatfield of Oregon. She also served as a research assistant to the House Committee on Education and Labor and as a press assistant to U.S. Representative Jeffrey Cohelan of California.